For TJS and Nathan

pricking balloons

*Varied voices cry
A pure symphony of hope,
All children blossom!

Cheers!
Jim*

poems by
JAMES C. MACDONALD

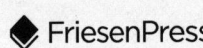

◆ FriesenPress

Suite 300 - 990 Fort St
Victoria, BC, V8V 3K2
Canada

www.friesenpress.com

Copyright © 2020 by James C. MacDonald
First Edition — 2020

All rights reserved.

No part of this publication may be reproduced in any form, or by any means, electronic or mechanical, including photocopying, recording, or any information browsing, storage, or retrieval system, without permission in writing from FriesenPress.

ISBN
978-1-5255-6559-5 (Hardcover)
978-1-5255-6560-1 (Paperback)
978-1-5255-6561-8 (eBook)

1. POETRY, CANADIAN

Distributed to the trade by The Ingram Book Company

For my sister, Shirley,
My loved ones lost,
and
My special muses
Who made these poems possible

Table of Contents

NEW ORLEANS I 1
   Fiction 2
   Crescent City Carnage 3
   Obituary 4
   Believe it or Not 5
   In Reflection 6
   Cain 7
   Lost Objects 8
   Identity 9
   The Daughters of Job 10
   The Little Girl in the Canal Street Mall 11
   The Seven Seals 12
   Janus Time 13

TORONTO AND RIDGEWAY 15
   Pricking Balloons 16
   The Fall 17
   The Devil 18
   Mad Song 19
   Fun House 20
   What the Spheres Said 21
   The Marriage 22
   Labyrinth 23
   The Occult 24
   The Possessed 25
   Reading for No Good Reason 26
   Miniature 27
   The Silent Desert 28

LAS VEGAS ... 29
- The Bet ... 30
- Las Vegas Panorama: From the Library at UNLV ... 31
- Chaos Theory ... 32
- Circus Circus ... 33
- Seeing Things ... 34
- Night Moods ... 35
- Dreamland ... 36
- Loss from Then to Now ... 37
- Society ... 38
- The Prophet ... 39
- Poetic Transformations ... 40
- Love Delayed ... 41
- Valentine I ... 42
- Valentine II ... 43
- Valentine III ... 44
- Lines on a Winter's Night ... 45
- Perplexed ... 46

NEW ORLEANS II ... 47
- Secret Gardens ... 48
- Wandering in the Quarter ... 49
- Looking Out onto Loyola ... 50
- Curiouser ... 51
- Selfies ... 52
- Pick a Stick at CC's Coffee House ... 53
- Anxiety ... 54
- Metamorphosis ... 55
- Illusion ... 56
- Giving Up the Night ... 57
- No Mean Feat ... 58
- Science: For Aristarchus ... 59
- The Wedding ... 60

ACKNOWLEDGEMENTS ... 61
ABOUT THE AUTHOR ... 63

New Orleans I

Mystery City

Fleeting clouds announcing Spring

Like shedding a mask

Fiction

What are these crude blots on a page
Real, or figments of my will,
Characters and myths truly pricked,
Or just some fractious notes fogging
My lonely writer's eye?

Crescent City Carnage
(Suspect dead, five bystanders wounded, February 17, 2019)

I see the Coca Cola truck pass by
Like others, steady, unaware of the carnage
Wrecked so recently on the bustling rues
Of this hazy crescent city.
Front page, of course, but not in bold colour
Like images of inexorable parades,
The daily Mardi Gras prefiguring
Lenten days and gods suffering
In the wilderness for spiritual insight,
Unlike the innocents standing around passive,
Unknowing, before being sprayed by lead,
Thinking more about beads than bullets.

JAMES C. MACDONALD

Obituary

Surprised, I look at those pages
Of the daily newspaper and
I'm struck by all the smiling faces
Staring resolutely from the
                      obituaries.
These figures are a shorthand look,
A simple message they were here
For such a short time, thinking, feeling
And changing, travelers trying to
                      embrace this life.
But the frozen, silent stares
Distance us from the heartfelt words
Of relatives, helpless in their loss,
Who can't explain the truth in those
                      cruel happy pictures.

Believe it or Not

Some of us are built for belief,
For others it is some relief
To avoid mystic promises with conviction
And just treat the occult as fiction.

Those skeptics who relish the thought
Of reality without the "ought,"
Unencumbered by traditional authority
Must be responsible without the duty.

Disciples on the other hand
Must construct their case and take a stand,
For an ethereal, not a myopic view
Of the fantastic but spiritually true.

But if arbiters try to judge
Which dilemma they don't begrudge,
They fail the human need to suit
An answer that is sadly moot.

JAMES C. MACDONALD

In Reflection

Was life like that
And now it's not,
A remembrance now passive
Of quotidian sighs
And vigorous thoughts,
Decisions made in intensity,
Knowing that time was infinite
And all error could be fixed,
Every offence mitigated
By conscious understanding,
But now in age we see
Each passing year watched with suspicion,
Common sense patchy and ephemeral,
Praise not for wisdom or truth
But for length of earthly service,
As enigmatic existence pitilessly
Treats us as mere bubbles
Flowing from a Mardi Gras balcony.

pricking balloons

Cain

Read your Midrash commentary
And speak loudly the truth of Cain,
Avoid the deadly homily;
Reify the true cause of pain.
Have the daring to face the page
In humble thought without the rage
Of priests abstractly guessing,
Healing their souls by confessing
To a higher power, summarily
Sentencing a youth without argument,
With enough strange guilt, authority sent,
To transience forced arbitrarily,
And this cruel gnomic choice
Has forever contrived
To silence his cries in deep plangent voice.

Lost Objects

In the caves at Qumran
Lost objects from a lost goat were found,
Words begetting controversies
As dogmatic then as now,
Sectarian wars supported by
Quibbling authorities.

In our perilous world
What was found seemed apocalyptic
To the testifying scholars
Who deny ancient context
And lecture to us, the common sheep
They so love.

Some foresee a modern day
Of atonement in these sacred words,
Their sectarian deity
Demanding total consent,
But maybe a witty god designs a cosmic joke
Puzzling us all to infinity.

Identity

Is there a secret message
In every public word
We dare to speak?

Outsiders translate these thoughts
Through their personal prisms
Changing the sense.

Is our conscious confusion
Now the true opposite of
Stunned Narcissus?

We see a petty riddle,
A puzzled smirk in the mirror,
A distortion.

Can we ever know for sure
How others see others' selves
With clarity?

Reflection on this response
Perpetuates a lasting
Anxiety.

Letting others interpret
Secrets, we journey unsafely
Beyond the self.

And in rejecting the self,
We let the world drive us
To melancholy.

The Daughters of Job

Forgive the daughters of Job,
Graced with inheritance and beauty,
Specifically named with identities
Not given their sisters,
Those struck down for a bet,
A metaphysical sparring made real.

In the end, did they question
Their sisters' roles in the game,
The suffering to prove a godly point,
Or did they carry on as usual
In a vacuum of experience,
A mere addendum to a horror story,
A lesson in obedience?

pricking balloons

The Little Girl in the Canal Street Mall

The little girl on the escalator,
A mere wisp with wobbly legs
Is taken by the hand forcefully
By her fearful father,
Who, with his mask of courage,
Seeks control for her safety
And his peace of mind,
Mistaking her jerky motions as frailty,
Not the daring effort
To coordinate her mind and body
By herself, on those convulsing stairs,
And she pulls away her hand, forcefully,
Teetering like on a tightrope,
Her father's mask now stripped off,
She, relishing the disobedience,
Feeling the power of independence,
And her father watches in horror,
His little girl jumping off upright
With a provocative smile of success
                    and defiance.

JAMES C. MACDONALD

The Seven Seals

What comes to pass as descending angels
And the dark witnesses to history,
With no insights nor magical trumpets,
Come to break the seals and halt despair?

They think they must seek divine knowledge
And read the sacred book to save the world,
But they will be shocked at empty pages,
Proving that the true light must be their own.

Janus Time

At a certain reflective age
In moments of lucidity,
The old can finally rage
At the world's gross timidity,
But any singular sage
Who dares claim this divinity
Must be a poet to beat the rhyme
And make sense of daily Janus time.

Toronto and Ridgeway

Varied voices choose
A pure symphony of hope
Through changing seasons

JAMES C. MACDONALD

Pricking Balloons

In that dreamland both night and day
On the cusp of worlds barely known,
The children smiling make their way
Needy, with thoughts and limbs half grown.

They play wildly in the mud
Whirling and whistling in their game,
Imagining free thoughts that yield
Treasures of feelings without name.

What do they like, what do they think,
Exploding balloons is their plan,
Young minds possessed when on the brink
Of reviving the great god Pan.

We all grow through experience
And all mortals grow up too soon,
But adults cringe most in defence
When kids love pricking balloons.

The Fall

Strange day awakening
From phantasmagoric dreamland
To morning absurdity, from
Godhead to kenosis, planning
To break into reality
And freedom on an empty stomach.

The imaginative world
Obviously isn't all Eden,
Or all excessive reflection,
The inner life contemplating
Its infinite possibilities.

No, I must eat that feared apple,
Not to gain pure knowledge of life,
But to feed my hunger despite
The sad results of not finding
Grave meaning in such a simple act.

The Devil

Smiling and open
He shakes hands
Gives a slight bow
And perhaps plants a mild
Kiss on a willing cheek.

He dresses well and speaks
Little, just enough to
Insinuate doubt, and then
Treads somewhere else
Having a very pleasant time.

Mad Song

It started as a child,
A misanthropic bent,
The need to be wild,
Then to and fro he went.

A smile disarmed,
A laugh beguiled,
He did charm us all,
In youthful style.

We accepted the lies,
We provided the hints,
We looked in his eyes
To find innocence.

We wanted to believe,
But couldn't conceive,
In one so swell,
The chilling glimpse of hell.

JAMES C. MACDONALD

Fun House

Fate, or whatever
Morning newspaper prophets
Call it now, resists easy
Explanation, like
Reflections in a parabolic mirror,
But it seems to be there
When we want it,
To get us off the hook
Of responsibility, like
Believing the images, not the object.

What the Spheres Said

In the distant harmony
Are sounds that are never heard
Never to be heard by those
Who live in stone,
Who see not the wind in the tree,
Who see not the cleansing fire,
Who care not.

The revolutions of the spirit
Are experiences never lived
Never to be lived by those
Who are made of straw,
Who fear the wind,
Who fear the fire,
Who feel not.

Past and present movements
Are explorations of the soul
Always to be known by those
Who dwell in freedom,
Who claim the wind,
Who breathe the fire,
Who dare to be.

The Marriage

Echoes of Cana heard again
In a distant land, transforming
Images of self into richer
Wine.

Alienated by a life
Of ritual passages, one
Finds finally the essence of
Rebirth.

And like water becomes itself
And more, the same miracle of
Self is regained in a truer
Bond.

pricking balloons

Labyrinth

Inside without
   direction
Wan der ing in perplexity,
Is it a search?
An emergence from doubt?
   Choices made
in frustration: What is
outside; is there an outside?
What monsters lie a-
Head in wait — Minotaurs
With double
Heads and bodies,
Heads and bodies
To swallow up thought, life,
   an end to perplexities or a
Beginning and knowledge already
Known.
Plod on out of interest and
   Me with no string.

The Occult

The cards have it all,
Love and death, the first
Things, the last things,
Prophecy and mystery with
The flick of a wrist.

Fear the hanged man,
Fear the beast within,
Fear the magician's hand,
Fear the tempter to sin.

Live with the cards
To create illusions
Which will come to pass,
Don't move without the knowledge,
It well may be your last.

The Possessed

Shadows invade the
Unparametered
Region, driving the
Light receding
Only as witness.

In the lumpen dark
Rahab looms to lead
The possessed, revived
By that common shame
Which knows no limits.

JAMES C. MACDONALD

Reading for No Good Reason

In the dictionary, I flit
"Morose, saturnine, lugubrious"—
No, those are just the words
On page 83.
But they don't mean anything to me,
Or do they become part of me,
Assimilated like light in the eye
Capturing all but some images
That dwell in the dictionary
In my brain.
"Lithoid," page 452.
Will I ever use it in
Conversation, as it is now
Embedded in my imagination,
Or is it soon forgotten also
Like life: more fleeting than flitting.

Miniature

Reduced by magic light
To pocket size
For carrying and possessing,
Passively,
The portrait is animated
Only by memory and wistful
Glances, which temporarily
Restore the spirit
From an instance
Once violently snapped.

JAMES C. MACDONALD

The Silent Desert

In that private land I exist,
Out of time, out of place,
Aboriginal perceptions confusing
Thought through Janus images.

Conjured gems to exorcize the devil,
Fail in the silence, defeating speculation
On consubstantiality again,
As I finally see the desert in a mirror.

Las Vegas

Is the coy serpent

A god trickster in disguise

Forever love's chaos

JAMES C. MACDONALD

The Bet

Dumb bet that Pascal,
Give up life now for eternal gains
On speculation, a philosophical
Lottery with no tangible reward
And no lightening of spiritual
Anguish.

A god, a god processing
Lottery tickets. Can the
Boredom be so great?

Las Vegas Panorama: From the Library at UNLV

Forty days and forty nights in this gaudy desert
Again, seeking some sort of enlightenment
Even in stubborn old age, focused on those
                            distant hills
Trying to make god's supposed artifact meaningful,
Invading the senses with eternity,
But reality intrudes through my wary
                            skeptic's eye
The whole, glowing spectacle once viewed from the fifth floor
Just reminds me of worlds beyond, just like this,
Trillions of light years glimpsed by the dreaming
                            human mind
Inventing that desert, those hills, inspired perhaps
By the mysterious divine artistry,
But finally, it is just the poet
                            on the page.

JAMES C. MACDONALD

Chaos Theory

Memory, is that all we know?
Minds like dead stars shining in the past;
Every now is then, so we create
Our meaning, often illusory.

Are others seen as just images?
Unsubstantial, fleeting, so perhaps
Unworthy of true commitment; we are
Fearful of the unpredictable.

Are we deceived by time's transience?
Or can we progress by some design,
A trick of mind to tame life's chaos
And proceed as if the present were real.

Circus Circus

Let's go to the Circus
    Every day
To see the motley freaks,
    The unpeople
To us solemn gawkers
    Circling them,
Risking our eternal souls
    For just a few laughs.

Let's see distorted lives
    Every day
To keep our sanity
    Firmly in check,
Silently affirming
    Our normalcy,
Without the consequences
    For just a few laughs.

Let us go home quickly
    Every day
With relief that tattoos,
    Indelible,
Would never wash off on us
    During our retreat.

Seeing Things

Seeing backwards is
Easier than seeing
Forwards; the images
Seem so true, but with
The distortion of
Time and its frivolous
Prismatic play.

Flash forward to what
We do wish to be true,
Pressing the past into
Life, an "ought to be"
Which exists as true until
It happens, and we make
Of it what we can.

Then and now equal and dangerous
Possibilities, the possibilities of
Poetry creating and recreating,
Hoping for some advantage.

Night Moods

Azrael, ambiguous angel, strides
Over me from youth to now, still,
In her Manichean mood resides,
Daring dark or bright as she will.

Some old, benign inner patterns she grants,
But often in my fretful dreams
Dangerous and mythic demons she plants,
Challenging me with all that seems.

Can I know now from her ancient insights,
And her ghouls with fever motions,
If my passions are mere appetites,
My fears just seductive illusions?

JAMES C. MACDONALD

Dreamland

Solitude threatens like pain
And night passes again,
Waking receding to dream,
Washed out illusions seem
Less trouble in colour.

But imagined escape makes
Infinite double takes,
The leap against thinking
Forces one into sinking
To unwanted depths of the self.

Loss from Then to Now

Loss, buried before, despite the grief
And appearance for the public,
Catatonic, world a dream vision;
Just go through the motions, zombie-like
Feelings rising from necessity
Strangling others, hoping to get close
But cannot, until age greets loss and
Suddenly, loneliness overwhelms,
Conjuring anew the spectral past
To make the repressed experience
Real again, all snug in the bones.

JAMES C. MACDONALD

Society

Why do the ones behind the mask
    Want a mask?
To be with the crowd, not alone
    With themselves,
And few see behind the façade
    Nor want to.

They all disappear in the crowd
    Seeking advice
From the authority they found,
    Hoping that
Abandoning the self will meet
    With approval.
These souls are not really hiding,
    They all think,
From the realities of life
    Beyond the mask,
Mesmerized as they are by the
    Rhetoric.

One with these masses, these leaders,
    Courting them
With hypnotic revelations
    Of the madness
Outside, charm them with their holy
    Infallibility.

pricking balloons

The Prophet

A prophet exists in all lands
In all times, calling his faithful
Around him like a vendor with wares,
Imparting wisdom.

They again set up his pedestal,
Each time a ritual, respect
For his age, and they circle him with love,
Courteous reverence.

Life demands a prophet, a glimpse
Of a future never known,
Always to be hoped for, but now hear
The wistful platitudes.

He sells his secret vision,
Homilies which might determine
Our futures, and a child, hearing,
Cries in discomfort.

Poetic Transformations

There exists in poetry a break of
Line, a caesura, analogous to
A pause of breath in harmonious song
To balance and sustain the metric mood.

Life in its discontinuity does
Reflect this seemingly artificial
Device, which implies the arbitrary
Nature of being, not the organic.

But the pause between two lives is much more
Than deliberate contrivance, and will
Be transformed, so await the miracles
Which once did haunt the hills of Galilee.

Love Delayed

Why here, why now?
Does distance matter
To mind and space.

Age is it now?
Not in play before,
Makes you near.

Is it real?
A surprise no doubt
To a skeptic.

Not mystical?
Just imagination
Poking about.

JAMES C. MACDONALD

Valentine I

Your light may be too much light,
It graces my world for now,
Enhancing my dull spirit,
But it can't last,
For it must inevitably
Turn to dark the life
That can't bear be near it.

Valentine II

The music sings its wild spell,
Seduces in a wisdom
Of feeling, so strong to be
Shaking the perceiving
Mind into loving thought.

I sang that song within me,
I remembered every note,
But time does now not spare me
And absence does remind me
The elusiveness of you.

Valentine III

How far it is from you to me
In place and time,
But short those long days past
When we met, a miracle, too short.
A lifetime would have helped,
But nature does what it will,
So scant years are enough
For me at least,
Embracing your spirit in wonder.

Lines on a Winter's Night

Frozen craft from an unseen hand
Signals the advent of deathly
Blankets of chilled crystal,
Descending harshly on fallen leaves
Completing their cruel submission.

Cocooned in artificial light,
I sit thinly distanced from those
Outside concerns, avoiding
The awful cycle and escaping
The prison of nature.

Perplexed

Is love both determined and free,
Or is it a matter of hot dispute?
Often confused, do we see
If our fate will bear rich fruit?

The question must always be there
Waiting an answer but now caught,
When life's roses say beware
Beauty with the prick of thought.

Your mystery does bind me, fraught
With love that might never be seen;
I am caught, so am I not
Pierrot to your Columbine?

New Orleans II

St. Louis # 1

Dances imperiously

Over droll Tremé

JAMES C. MACDONALD

Secret Gardens

Wandering the rutted lanes
Of this mysterious Quarter,
Eyes not penetrating
The shuttered cottages
Flush almost to the cracked rues,
Colorful and charming
But seemingly impenetrable
Until a flash of green
Or orange or red or yellow
Beckons through a grate, a portal,
Surprising verdure beyond the facades
Of life we can't know there,
Wild or cultivated,
A courtyard, a garden, a tree,
Overgrown slave quarters, a retreat?
Just glimpses of
Vermillion splashes over boxwood hedges,
Lavender wisteria blessing our senses,
Transforming our imaginations
To visions of the sun,
Pouring light on hidden spaces,
Our ancient curiosity once more
Thirsting for intimate knowledge
Of these minor Edens,
But with no invitations to access,
Our loss reminds us only of
The true genesis of secrecy.

Wandering in the Quarter

While on Bourbon Street,
She asked where I was going,
And I said somewhat automatically,
                               Nowhere,
So perhaps sensing an annihilating
    Personality,
She went another way, not disgusted but
    Perplexed.

Turning on to Conti
Feeling alienated,
I then reflected on my situation,
    What now?

Did I consciously know that I was going
    In some direction
That my elusive self created
    Unperplexed?

JAMES C. MACDONALD

Looking Out onto Loyola

This window is like a moving photograph,
A glass wall seen through to a new world
Every minute in colour and light,
Humanity evolving, never static,
Going somewhere often without design
And I feel safe, temporarily,
But chill when wondering
At how fleeting and unstoppable
Is this panorama.

pricking balloons

Curiouser

From the Garden to one life of that cat,
Modern Bluebeards still view curiosity
As the one evil, refusing pardon
For their convenience when conscience fails,
Who justify their sterile grievances
By fantasizing that Eve's heroic act
Was the original and future sin,
Forever creating naïve victims,
Punished unwittingly for unlocking
The secret doors to reason and knowledge.
So, like Eve, when defying myth sophists,
Who win only when the truth hibernates,
Never forget that the cat has eight more lives.

JAMES C. MACDONALD

Selfies

The pilgrims come to this mystic city
Looking for themselves
In their mirror phones,
Hoping for virtues bounced
Onto their rictal faces,
And like the Lordes of ancient Aachen,
Coveting holy relics,
Deceived by the cheerful smithies
Peddling metallic reflections,
These modern naifs,
Strangling their narcissistic cells
Expose themselves as another nimbus of fools.

pricking balloons

Pick a Stick at CC's Coffee House

Every day I pick a stick
To stir my hot coffee,
A choice at once algebraic,
At times mental dystrophy.

Should I choose the one jumping out,
Maybe placed there to nudge
A Frostian thinker to doubt
The worth of a mind to judge.

I am conscious how contingent
Is this selection ever small,
Just another arcane event
Keeping my peevish will in thrall.

In these realms often tentative,
To be so metaphysical
Destines thoughts not definitive
To pages mostly whimsical.

Anxiety

The modern world spins,
But suddenly it stops
As in ages before,
Begetting the fog life
Of the Cimmerians,
Absolute in tragic
Darkness of mind and soul,
Jealously guarding the
Discovery of light,
Not with the crude weapons
Of mass destruction,
But with planting fear
In all who dare create
Life giving radiance.

Metamorphosis

The butterfly will still not settle
Upon nettles,
Fearing them in the past at
Another stage,
Not out of vanity
Instead, purity.

Ecclesiastes is vanity
To make decree
Causing fear to anxious youth,
Conforming to past rules
To quash the fools.

The caterpillar now transfigures
With harsh rigours
Of spite for self righteous laws
Made by preachers,
So will come to freedom
Through its own wisdom.

Illusion

They say everything happens for a reason
The four last things
All the first things
Children of light
Children of dark
A smile, a flinch, a tear
A cloud, a flood
Sunlight,
The politician who elicits Kentish fire
For brutish speech
And acolytes who seek to burn witches
Found everywhere
In this modern world,
And people who want to believe
In something,
Even deception,
And feel better enduring a holocaust
For something that designs for a reason
The good, the bad
The entropic, the resurrection,
Otherwise, who could survive this chaos
Of life, love, and death,
Who could whip the holy innocents,
Except those embracing the awful
Truth of existence.

pricking balloons

Giving Up the Night

Once more I drift into the night,
Confronting the fading of the light,
Shadows in the alleys of my mind
Conjuring up the demon kind.

This Lilith time shakes my being,
Since I have no fear when seeing,
But sight when lost to astral dark
Makes lurid dreams that much more stark.

These black depths do make me aware
Of the thing that invokes nightmare,
A succubus which floats with glee,
Charging her devilish, exacting fee.

Each slow dawn is welcomed with relief
As firefly dance renews belief
That memory finds more fruitful ways
To expel dark moon haunting days.

JAMES C. MACDONALD

No Mean Feat

Some thought him a bold magician,
For on that searing summer's day
He brought water from the desert,
An unheard-of feat in those times
When rain waited in the heavens
For a chosen son of thunder
To fertilize this barren land.

But he was no hero magus,
Just an ordinary fellow
Who knew where to look, insight gained
Through his travels, understanding
Nature and demystifying
The falsities of ritual
That pass for scientific thought.

Science: For Aristarchus

Steady the sun,
Small fire hidden
By a finger
Of the mythic ones,
Waiting the sinking
Of light to darkness,
Unknowing why the change,
Movement a mystery
For life giving, a god
Exempt from blasphemy,
And worshipped by nescient priests,
Until in Samos foresight
Prevailed against condemnation
And the sun grew, and the earth moved
Gracefully around the reified blaze.

JAMES C. MACDONALD

The Wedding

They stand mostly tall and smart
At the Hotel Monteleone,
Awaiting an old-time wedding to start,
The bride nervous but can't postpone.

Hotel guests scurry about oblivious
To the sacramental ritual;
To the secret watcher, though, it's obvious
That people are habitual.

And whatever qualms exist,
Despite modern skeptics' distress,
Traditions will ever persist,
For a new life of happiness.

Acknowledgements

I would like to thank the team at FriesenPress, led by Liza Weppenaar who always provided clarity and welcome help when needed. Also, I am grateful to Kurt Hershey for his wonderful cover illustration and to Janine for an astute job of editing. Thanks to Debby and Tony Sacino for expertly dealing with a challenging manuscript and Tim Currah for his technical expertise. Special thanks to Shirley and Bill Hawkey for all their support at crucial times on this journey.

About the Author

James C. MacDonald was Professor and Associate Dean of English at Humber College in Toronto. He was educated at Waterloo Lutheran University and the University of Toronto. As editor, writer, and consultant, he has worked for many publishing companies, the Canadian Institute for the Administration of Justice, and government agencies such as CIDA and APEC. He has also published various articles on education and Canadian and British literature. He now spends his time in the Niagara Region and New Orleans.

Printed in Canada